D0667619

PERFECT LAWNS

Simon Akeroyd

National Trust

First published in the United Kingdom in 2019 by
National Trust Books
43 Great Ormond Street
London
WC1N 3HZ

An imprint of Pavilion Books Company Ltd

ISBN 978-1-91135-872-5

A CIP catalogue record for this book is available from the British Library.

10 9 8 7 6 5 4 3 2 1

Reproduction by Mission Productions Ltd, Hong Kong
Printed and bound by 1010 Printing International Ltd, China

This book can be ordered direct from the publisher at www.pavilionbooks.com

Interior illustrations by Abi Read

CONTENTS

Introduction
4

Creating a lawn
6

Maintaining your lawn
38

Troubleshooting
76

Index
96

INTRODUCTION

The lawn sometimes seems like a peculiarly British obsession. Whether we think of Edwardian ladies taking tea on the lawn, or grandfathers mowing every Sunday, whether we watch or play football, cricket, tennis or rugby, grass looms large in our heritage and collective memory. Ours is a green and pleasant land, after all, a place where children grow up making daisy chains and young lovers decide their fate with a handful of petals.

Yet recently lawns have had a rather bad press. The classic lawn, mowed constantly, watered and fed unnaturally and often sprayed with a variety of chemicals, comes in for much criticism from ecologists and no longer fits the modern, more natural, environmentally friendly zeitgeist. So it is rather ironic that we are increasingly ripping up grass only to replace it with concrete, decking or gravel, surfaces that do not benefit the environment in any way and actually do more harm than grass ever can. Even the most perfectly striped and managed lawn consumes carbon dioxide, produces oxygen and absorbs both heat and rain. That is surely better than a patch of ugly concrete, and certainly a lot more pleasant to walk on.

In any case there is no requirement for a lawn to fit this traditional mould. The modern 'perfect' lawn is one that is perfect for you: for your needs, your lifestyle, your philosophy, your hobbies, for whatever way you choose to live. It can be a tiny box of turf on your city flat balcony; it can cover the roof of a shed; it can be an easy-to-care-for meadow full of wildlife and interest; or it can just be an extra green-carpeted space for your children to play on.

In most cases lawns are still the perfect way to provide the essential space that allows us to get on with tasks and activities outside. Their versatility and usefulness makes them the undisputed centre of the garden, so knowing how best to look after them and keep them in good condition is both critically important and rewarding.

So this book is all about lawns, in all their varied forms. Whether big or small, the same techniques of lawn care and maintenance apply.

CREATING A LAWN

LAWN TYPES

From the pocket-handkerchief lawns of small front gardens to the great swathes of grass surrounding a stately home, lawns come in all shapes and sizes. Their design, shape and style are a result of a wide range of factors, but creating or developing your lawn is as dependent on your creative imagination as it is on your practical needs.

Formal lawns

A good formal lawn will require plenty of regular maintenance, but it can be an impressive sight if looked after correctly. Given that the lawn is often the single largest part of a garden it may even become its most important feature in its own right. Formal lawns will bring a quiet dignity to your garden, providing a strong, delineated framework for the flowing lines of traditional flower borders or more symmetrical geometric beds. They are ideally placed close to the house where they can be easily admired and look best when the lines are clean and the shape well-defined. Getting the look will take some effort and time but is easier to achieve than one might think.

Family/utility lawns

Today's gardens often have to perform a multitude of roles. Increasingly we treat them as an outside room as well as an outside utility area. If life is busy, time at a premium and children, dogs and other family members are around, you want a lawn that is robust enough to handle regular use. That does not mean, though, that it cannot be interesting. Grass mixes that can withstand the constant wear and tear, carefully placed stepping stones and hard landscaping, winding paths and irregular shapes can help to create a useful but fun environment to relax and play in.

Non-grass lawns

At either end of the 'lawn' spectrum there are plenty of options that exclude the use of grass, or limit the mowing of it at least. Artificial turf once had a bad reputation and a very definitely plastic look, but today's manufacturers have worked hard to create a more natural feel. It may be the perfect option for those who have neither the time nor conditions to keep a grass lawn in shape, as well as helping hay fever sufferers cope in summer.

Other options can be much friendlier to wildlife. Long grass or wildflower meadows need mowing much less regularly and will provide food and shelter to a host of insects, birds and mammals, and will also add movement, texture and colour to your garden design. Or you could choose a green lawn that has no grass at all. Chamomile is a popular choice. It is soft and cushiony and smells wonderful. Clover lawns retain their green even in times of drought, while mind-your-own-business (*Soleirolia soleirolii*) will merrily cover damp, shady areas with a carpet of dense, tiny leaves in mild conditions, but can become very invasive given half a chance.

One or other type of lawn may be exactly what suits you, but it does not follow that you have to stick only to this one type. The best gardens are those that fulfil a variety of needs and there is no limit other than your own imagination to creating different lawns in different places.

DESIGNING LAWNS

Exploring options and being realistic about your needs before you actually create your lawn will save you a great deal of time and trouble later on. Begin by listing your requirements and preferences, and use this information to make a rough sketch of where you want to put your lawn and how it will combine with the rest of the garden before you pick up your spade. You will need to think about the following.

Size and shape

How much of your garden you want as lawn depends on three major factors: how much space you have, how often you will be using it for practical purposes, and how much time you will have to look after it. Straight edges and formal lines will need more constant maintenance to look good, as will turf seats, grass incorporated into living walls, and any other creative ideas you may come up with.

If you would like a lawn that is spacious but still want plenty of shrubs and flowers to enjoy, avoid placing skinny borders around each lawn edge. Instead, try to add a more flowing, intriguing shape on one or two sides. One wider border is much more interesting and will reduce the need to constantly cut back border plants and shrubs that will inevitably grow outwards and shade the lawn if there is not enough space.

Surrounding features

Houses, trees and other tall structures can have a huge impact on lawns, sheltering areas from the sun or rain, so they need to be taken into account in the design process. Deciduous trees drop their leaves in autumn, and they may need clearing off lawns to keep them looking smart. Evergreens create a shady and dry atmosphere underneath their dense canopy. Conifer needles especially can create a huge problem, as their acidity and chemical composition deters grass from growing underneath.

On a more positive note, lawns are a wonderful way to lead the eye to any focal points and features you want to show off.

Access

Access is an important consideration, as a well-used lawn will get muddy in the colder and wetter months. Bins, sheds, compost heaps and washing lines should all be easily accessible, so consider whether a path in a lawn or stepping stones might be required. Garden furniture such as dining sets and loungers, as well as children's play equipment, will also create extra wear and tear and, if wooden, will rot if placed directly onto grass, so think carefully when designing round such garden additions.

Sustainability

Considering the impact of your gardening activities on the wider environment is becoming increasingly important. Whether you want to encourage a better environment for wildlife or simply reduce your environmental footprint, you can choose a variety of lawn options that suit your purpose.

PREPARATION BASICS

Drainage and soil condition

To achieve success, laying a new lawn, like so much in life, requires planning and preparation.

The first step in creating a lawn, or renovating an old shabby one, is to clear the ground. You can either use a weedkiller to kill off any weeds, plants and old turf, or dig the ground over thoroughly, paying special attention to the roots of perennial weeds such as dock and dandelion. If you are renovating an area that has previously existed as a lawn it is easier to slice the remaining turf away first before attempting to dig. Even if sprayed it will need removing separately, as grass roots form a thick mat that is difficult to chop in.

Next, leave the ground for a few weeks, before removing any regrowth that appears.

The ideal conditions for a lawn are a well-drained site with around 20cm (8in) of sandy, loamy topsoil over a free-draining subsoil. This means that the grass has plenty of root space to delve deep for essential nutrients and minimises the chance of waterlogged soil, which harms both plants and footwear. At first glance this may appear a little technical, but it is easier to understand step by step, and you are unlikely to have to take every possible action to achieve a good result.

As prevention is always better than cure, now is the time to put necessary measures in place to compensate for less than ideal conditions. Soil testing kits are easily available and will help you determine whether you need to adjust your soil for pH or fertility, and digging an exploratory pit will help you determine the makeup of the ground beneath.

PROBLEM	ACTION REQUIRED
Acidic soil	Add lime
Heavy clay soil	Add organic material and sand
Sandy soil	Add organic material
Infertile, poor soil	Add organic material and fertiliser
Shallow soil	Remove subsoil and replace with topsoil
Stony soil	Remove as many stones as possible by hand or garden rake

In a very few cases where the ground is extremely waterlogged it may be worth adding a drainage system below the level of the topsoil. A herringbone system of porous pipes to drain water away or a layer of gravel and sand might be a solution, albeit time-consuming, expensive and probably requiring the services of a professional. It will, however, prevent numerous problems appearing later on, which will either frustrate and spoil your dreams of a perfect lawn or require constant remedial work.

Add any additional materials to the soil before digging over or rotavating the area. Keep removing stones,, weeds and roots as they appear.

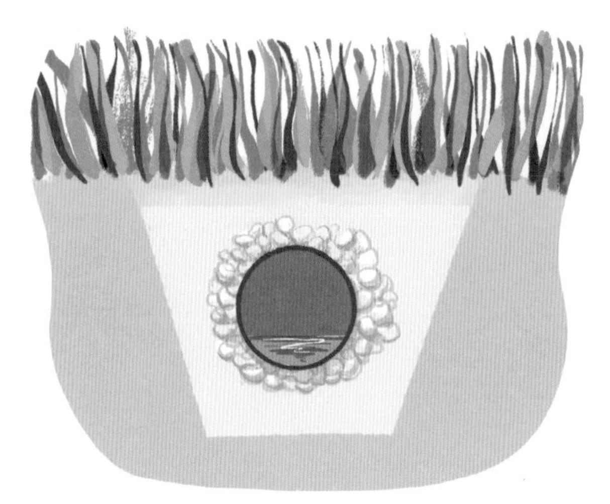

Cross section of a porous pipe dug into the ground to help with severe waterlogging.

Levelling

In most cases the area set aside for a lawn will contain only minor lumps and bumps which can be raked out relatively easily and the topsoil will be a pretty standard depth throughout the site. The more informal an area is the less levelling will be needed. In the case of meadows or long grass, it is hardly required at all, as a little natural variation adds to the informal effect.

Levelling as a rule is a fairly simple task. A big landscape rake will save time if smoothing out a large expanse, but a standard garden rake will do just as well and is all that is required for a small area. Pull the rake backwards and forwards to break up bigger clods of earth and to even out the soil level.

For more formal lawns, lawns that are to be used for specific sports, and landscapes that have a considerable variation in height or are distinctly sloped, a slightly more complicated technique will probably be required.

To achieve the most accurate levels you will need a number of pre-marked pegs, each one marked at the same distance from the top. These are knocked into the ground in a grid formation to the same depth at equal distance from each other. Lay a plank along each row with a spirit level balanced on top and check that the pegs are all the same height, then add or remove topsoil until each peg is buried up to the mark.

If you are planning to turf rather than seed your lawn, ensure that the level is 2cm (¾in) below its final required level to leave space for the turf itself.

A similar technique is used for creating or smoothing out slopes, using pegs that are marked further up or down to create a gradual gradient. In extreme cases, if large amounts of ground are being moved, remove all the topsoil first and grade the subsoil before replacing the topsoil, or you will end up with a base that is too shallow at the bottom and too deep at the top.

Pegs are the best method of ensuring an even, level surface.

FINAL PREPARATIONS

Once you are happy with the drainage and levels and are confident that the ground is weed-free and as stone-free as possible, it is time to make the final preparations before sowing or turfing your perfect lawn.

Firming and raking

Tread gently over the cleared area to firm the soil and remove any air pockets, or use the back of a rake in a smaller area to achieve the same effect. The treading technique should be more of a shuffle than a stomp, as that will only compress the soil. Make sure the soil is dry as it will compact if wet and its structure will be damaged.

Next, rake the surface to create what is known as a fine tilth. The end result should be no clumps or large stones and a fine surface that grass seeds or turf roots will bed into with a minimum of effort.

Fertilising grass lawns

A few days before seeding or turf laying, add a granular fertiliser to the soil. This will give your new lawn a head start in its early days.

A balanced fertiliser that contains nitrogen, phosphorus and potassium is more than adequate for most lawns and soil conditions. For organic gardeners pelleted chicken manure is a good choice, while for non-organic gardeners there is a range of granular compounds available that contain the necessary nutrients in balanced quantities. In both cases apply at the manufacturer's recommended rate to avoid scorching newly established grass. Specialist lawn fertilisers are also available, although they are usually more expensive and also need to be applied in exact quantities.

Any fertiliser applied should be gently raked into the top few centimetres, without disturbing the level of the soil too much.

Preparing meadows

Unlike grass, most meadow flowers thrive in soil that is poor and much less fertile. So rather than add fertiliser and topsoil to the site it may be more suitable to avoid any kind of fertiliser at all. It will only encourage and feed the weeds and coarse grasses that outcompete most meadow flowers. If the topsoil in situ is already fertile, perhaps having being used for vegetable gardening in the past, it might even be wise to remove the top few centimetres to create shallower, poorer conditions.

TO TURF OR NOT TO TURF?

There is more than one way to create a lawn from scratch. Each method has its advantages and disadvantages so it is up to you to decide which one works for you. You could also decide to go for long grass or a meadow.

Seed

Advantages

* Usually the cheapest option.
* Grass seed and meadow mixes can be mixed to suit conditions. Specialist mixes are available for shade, damp, drought resistance, woodland, coasts and any manner of conditions. With a bit of research you can mix and match your own seed to suit your local conditions exactly.
* Does not require much physical strength.
* Seed will keep for a while if sowing conditions are not right.

Disadvantages

* Takes longer to establish.
* Cannot be walked on for a period of time after sowing.
* Requires regular watering initially.
* Usually only successful in spring and autumn as grass will not germinate if temperatures are too low or high.
* May need to be protected from birds.

Turf

Advantages

* Can be laid pretty much all year round.
* Can be walked on after just a few days of laying.
* Gives an instant result – a lush greensward straight away.

Disadvantages

* More expensive.
* Has to be unrolled and laid quickly as it will start to heat up and compost if left stacked.
* Turf rolls can be heavy and will take some effort to move.

Meadows and long grass

Advantages

* Long grass requires less mowing, reducing the use of fuel and your carbon footprint.
* Meadows help to increase biodiversity in your garden.
* Bee-friendly meadows are disappearing in the countryside so having one in your garden may help the bee population along with many other pollinators.

Disadvantages

* Once a year at least meadows and long grass have to be cut back and the hay disposed of.
* Can look messy, especially long grass.
* Not good for people who suffer from hay fever or other allergies.
* There is no guarantee any flowers will reproduce and produce seed from one year to the next, giving a patchy effect.
* Perennial weeds such as thistle and ragwort will creep in over time and are difficult to remove.

CREATING A LAWN FROM SEED

Prepare the area to be sown as described on page 17.

Try to pick a day with little or no wind, since grass seed is extremely light and easily blown away. The seed will germinate most quickly and successfully in warm, moist conditions so spring and autumn are the best times to sow, although cooler summers may be an option, as long as plenty of irrigation is available.

As a rule of thumb, autumn-sown seed is more successful than that sown in spring, the soil having been warmed up over summer, but the difference in germination success is relatively minor.

For sowing by hand first divide the area to be sown into 1m (3ft) squares using canes or string. Measure out the correct quantity of grass seed for each square according to the manufacturer's instructions or at roughly 25–50g per m^2 depending on the coarseness of the grass. A small paper cup makes an ideal container.

Divide each measure into two, then evenly scatter the first half over the entire square before sowing the second half at 90° from the original direction. Try to keep the distribution as even as possible.

Repeat for each marked-out square. Once all the seed has been sown, gently rake the seed in so that it is mostly just covered by the soil.

Unless rain is guaranteed, water using a watering can with an upside-down rose to avoid washing away seed, or with a hosepipe attached to a sprinkler or spray attachment. Germination should take around 1–3 weeks depending on the species of grass sown and weather conditions.

Mark out areas for sowing to ensure even seed distribution.

For larger areas a seed spreader will save a lot of time and measuring as, if calibrated correctly, it will drop the seed much more evenly and quickly. A sheet or tarpaulin laid over areas that you do not wish to grass will help keep edges neat and tidy.

Care in the first few weeks

Birds can be a real problem when it comes to newly sown lawns, so prevent them from raiding your grass seed by covering it with black netting or brushwood. Old shiny CDs hung from poles will also help as they flash in sunlight and many birds find this disturbing. Remove any protection as soon as the seed has successfully germinated to ensure that the newly emerged seedlings have maximum access to sunlight.

Keep the seeds and seedlings well watered for the first month or so, especially if no rain falls, as germinating seeds and young grass seedlings are very susceptible to drought and can easily die.

Once the seedlings have emerged some gardeners like to gently firm the soil with a light roller, to flatten down the tiny breaks and cracks in the soil that the emerging seedlings create, though this practice is now somewhat out of fashion.

Seeded grass can be cut once it has reached about 5cm (2in) high. Reduce the height by half, ideally with a rotary rather than a cylinder mower, as this ensures less tearing of the young blades, then remove the clippings by raking gently.

As time goes by and the grass establishes, the height of the cut can be gradually reduced and different mowers can be used.

LAYING A TURF LAWN

Turf is available in several shapes and sizes, ranging from high-quality rolls cut from commercial turf fields to shorter lengths of rougher, more agricultural field grass. It is even sometimes possible to buy turf that is suitable for shade or damp conditions. If you happen to be a Premiership football club then you will be able to afford to buy turf especially grown for your pitch, but most people have to take their pick of what is available locally.

Ideally turf should be laid within 24 hours of being lifted, so do buy it from a reputable source: if left for any longer it will either dry out or begin to compost. Older turf will look yellow and feel hot as a result of the composting process. If there is a delay, unroll each piece, lay it flat, grass side up, and away from strong sunlight. Water frequently to keep it in good condition.

Once you've prepared the ground correctly, laying turf should be a fairly simple process.

If possible, start at a straight edge and unroll or lay each piece of turf as close as possible to one another. Kneeling on a plank will prevent any unintentional indentations appearing on the turf.

Stagger the joins on the next row along, like brickwork, to create a sturdier lawn. It is better to lay larger pieces along any edges and place small ones towards the middle as this will prevent these smaller bits drying out too quickly.

Kneeling on a plank helps keep turf neat and smooth as you are laying it.

Once all the pieces are laid, tamp down each piece with the back of a rake to ensure good contact with the soil underneath, and trim any unwanted pieces.

After this, brush a sandy top dressing into any cracks and gaps with a broom or besom until no longer visible.

Water the turf deeply immediately after laying to encourage the roots to grow downwards into the underlying soil.

Unlike seeded lawns, turf can be walked on after a few days, and can be cut with a mower as soon as it has clearly established.

FINAL TURF-LAYING TOUCHES

Shaping

To achieve a clean, straight line, use a taut string and plank as a guide. Trim any unwanted turf using a sharp spade or edging iron.

For curves use a flexible pipe or tube pinned into the ground in the right shape – a hosepipe is ideal – and trim away any turf outside it.

For a perfect circle, first mark out a square with string and pegs to check the overall size that you wish it to be. Stretch the string from one corner to the opposite corner and repeat with the two remaining corners to find the centre.

Using this centre make a compass with a peg and a length of string and draw out the circle, ensuring that it meets the square on each of the four sides. Mark with sand or marking paint and cut around this shape with an edging iron. Lift the unwanted turf with a spade in small sections and compost.

For completing planting circles within a lawn follow the same process but cut away the turf within the line.

Edging

It is not essential to use edging around a lawn, but it will create a neater finish and makes tidying and mowing a lot easier.

Wooden edging panels, treated against rot, will give a slightly rustic feel and are useful for straight edges between lawns and borders, as are stone edges, which will give a more formal look.

Creating curves is easy if you mark out the shape with a hosepipe.

Bricks laid side by side and slightly lower than the level of the lawn for easy mowing are another option that gives a good clean edge. Alternatively they can be laid angled on their sides to create a diamond effect.

For curves and circles, flexible edging, usually plastic, is the most useful option. Shaped metal edging can perform the same function and will last much longer, but this is definitely a more expensive choice.

Inserting stepping stones

Stepping stones can help to reduce wear and tear in areas of high traffic as well as leading the eye to focal points or showing the way to interesting parts of the garden.

Lay them out first to ensure they are easy to walk over without striding before cutting round them with a sharp knife.

Remove the cut turf using a spade and trowel away enough of the soil underneath to ensure that the paving will eventually sit just below the level of the grass – this ensures the mower will travel smoothly over any stones without being damaged.

Level the soil and put down a layer of sand, tamped down firmly, before placing the paving slab on top. Use mortar to fix the paving slabs or stones in place for a more permanent result.

Lawns do not have to be made of grass. Ground cover plants can be just as successful.

NON-GRASS LAWN OPTIONS

Creeping ground cover plants

While grass is undoubtedly the most popular choice for creating a lawn, there is no reason why other plants cannot be considered, especially in smaller areas that are off the beaten track of the garden. The most popular and romantic option is to use chamomile. Its creeping nature covers the ground well and it releases the most delicious scent when walked upon. It also feels wonderful under bare feet. For a restful design, inspired by Japanese gardens, moss, in damp, shady positions, is incredibly stylish and beautiful, though tricky to pull off successfully.

White clover (*Trifolium repens*) lawns are also becoming increasingly popular as a more sustainable alternative to traditional grass. Clover lawns are good for biodiversity and require little or no mowing. They also withstand harsh conditions such as poor soil and drought much better than most grass, can cope with dog urine and need no extra fertilisation as they fix their own nitrogen. Clover lawns are easily grown from seed.

Other plants that will create extra interest and texture include low-growing thyme, again scented and perfect for dry, sunny spaces, while mind-your-own-business (*Soleirolia soleirolii*) is a good option for damp, sheltered areas. If you have no intention at all of walking over a particular space, then the list of possible plants expands dramatically – periwinkle, lily of the valley, heather, and even sedums and houseleeks planted *en masse*, can look wonderful and will certainly ring the changes.

Planting a chamomile lawn

The best variety of chamomile to use for a lawn is the non-flowering 'Treneague', which is only available from cuttings or as plug plants.

To plant, prepare the ground as for any planting, i.e. dig thoroughly, fertilise and weed. Plant each rooted cutting or plug around 10cm (4in) apart and water in well. Keep well watered in dry spells and only walk on this kind of lawn occasionally, since it is not as robust as grass.

For other types of plants grown as a lawn, follow the same maintenance regime as if in a border.

NATURALISTIC PLANTING FOR WILDLIFE

Long grass, meadows and bulbs

However smart a mown grass lawn looks, it is, by its very nature, a poor choice for those who want to encourage biodiversity in the garden. The constant mowing regime prevents flowers and seeds forming and these are essential food sources for a wide variety of insects and birds. A weed-free lawn is also a monoculture, the scourge of the modern ecologist, for whom diversity is key, and if kept short provides no shelter for any mammals and other creatures that want to remain hidden from the beady eyes of predators.

The perfect grass lawn for wildlife, therefore, is one left to grow naturally and contains a variety of native weeds and other plants. Your neighbours may have something to say about this, and it may be a step too far to allow your garden to become a complete wildlife sanctuary at the expense of any horticulture, but there may be small areas that you are happy to leave pretty much to their own devices, perhaps away from the house and prying, judgemental eyes. Most grasses look rather wonderful when their seedheads are swaying in the breeze, and what you lose in neatness you will gain in movement, life and ease of maintenance. Allowing grass to grow long requires little or no effort. You may even find some interesting native flowers appearing from nowhere.

Flower meadows are an excellent choice for areas where the soil is poor as they are traditionally made up of flowers suited to difficult conditions where other plants would fail. Low fertility is a prerequisite, so there is no need to spend time improving the

soil beforehand. If anything you may have to reduce fertility, either by removing topsoil or by a long-term regime of mowing and removing clippings for several years in established grassland, such as under orchard trees, to ensure success.

If you are planning to sow from scratch, the same preparations as for turf or grass sowing apply, the only difference being in the reduction of soil fertility and in the quantities of seed sown.

The easiest way to establish a flower meadow is to sow seed into bare ground. A mix of annuals should flower the same year and provide impact in as little as six weeks from sowing, but perennial mixtures made up of flower and grass seed are also available, which will establish more slowly but provide a longer-term display.

Wildflower seeds tend to be much lighter in weight and they are often tiny, so it is useful to mix some fine sand in with the seed mixture to make sowing easier. Follow the manufacturer's instructions as to the correct amounts, as wildflower mixtures vary much more than grass mixes do.

Thereafter follow the same steps as for a grass lawn, watering and protecting from birds until germination. It is worth noting that a flower meadow sown in autumn will flower much earlier than a meadow sown in spring.

In larger areas of the garden it may not be possible to remove all the existing vegetation so various options are possible. You could clear individual small patches and sow meadow flowers into the bare patches, or, alternatively, mow areas short before planting plug plants into the cleared spaces. You could also try sowing

Add wildflowers to your lawn to create colour and interest.

yellow rattle (*Rhinanthus minor*) into any existing grasses several years before trying to grow meadow flowers. This parasitic meadow flower attaches to the roots of nearby grasses and reduces their vigour so that meadow plants have a better chance of establishing.

Avoid planting too symmetrically or geometrically as this looks unnatural. Try and inject some randomness into the design. For an up-to-date and stylish look, mow wide paths through your meadow to make it easier to access and admire.

Flowers to try in an annual meadow

* Common poppy (*Papaver rhoeas*)
* Opium poppy (*Papaver somniferum*)
* Common sunflower (*Helianthus annuus*)
* Cornflower, bachelor's button (*Centaurea cyanus*)
* Corn chamomile (*Anthemis arvensis*)
* Corn marigold (*Glebionis segetum*)
* Corn cockle (*Agrostemma githago*)

Flowers to try in a perennial meadow

* Meadow cranesbill (*Geranium pratense*)
* Field scabious (*Knautia arvensis*)
* Ox-eye daisy (*Leucanthemum vulgare*)
* Common yarrow (*Achillea millefolium*)
* Common cowslip (*Primula veris*)
* Primrose (*Primula vulgaris*)

Bulbs

Bulbs too are a super choice for naturalising in grass, extending interest outside the main flowering period of the garden and offering diversity with little effort.

For small quantities of bulbs a bulb planter is more than adequate. It is standard practice to scatter the bulbs gently over the ground and to plant them where they land to ensure the final effect is natural-looking. Take out a plug of soil with the bulb planter, add a small quantity of sand if the soil is heavy and place the bulbs the right way up in the hole at a depth of around twice their height. Backfill the hole and replace the plug of turf.

For a larger number of bulbs cut out squares or rectangles using an edging iron, slice under the turf horizontally and peel it back. Loosen the soil underneath before scattering bulbs and planting at the appropriate depth. Roll the turf back over and firm with the back of a rake.

For a more manicured look, create pockets of bulbs, leaving adequate space between them, and mow the areas in between as usual.

Bulbs suitable for naturalising in grass

* Petticoat daffodil (*Narcissus bulbocodium*)
* Snowdrop (*Galanthus nivalis*) (especially under trees)
* Crocus cultivars (spring- and autumn-flowering)
* Snake's head fritillary (*Fritillaria meleagris*)

NON-GRASS OPTIONS

Artificial turf

Artificial turf has come a long way from the stiff, green, spiky plastic coverings that used to be seen on the greengrocer's display stand. Modern products are soft and natural-looking, engineered to replicate real grass without the hard work that looking after a living lawn entails. They can make any outdoor space more usable whatever the weather conditions. Its major drawback, of course, is that it is completely sterile, making no contribution to biodiversity or to the crucial role that plant life has on our planet and air quality.

Sports pitches around the country are now increasingly artificial, allowing much greater use throughout the year as well as preventing mud and dirt ending up on sportswear. This is also a major consideration for homes with children and pets. Artificial turf is a useful option for those with limited mobility or who may be simply unable to manage a real lawn.

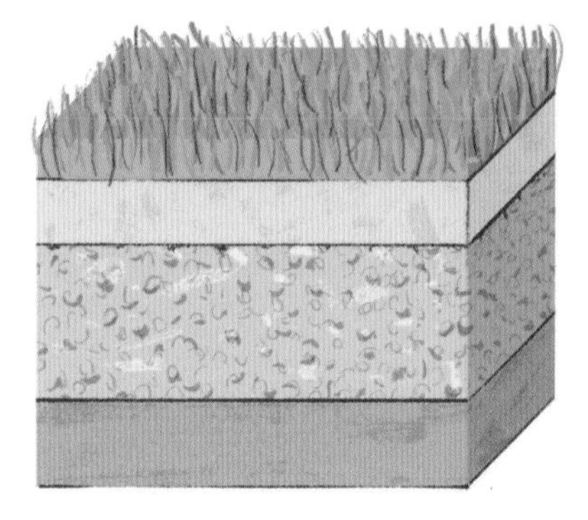

Artificial turf is laid over various different materials that help provide a stable base.

Laying artificial turf

Remove any existing turf and perennial weeds before digging out soil to a depth of 4–6cm (1½–2½in).

Lay a sheet of weed-suppressing membrane over the area before applying a thin layer of crushed stone or grit. Once compacted this will provide a stable, well-drained base.

Follow this with a layer of sharp sand. This too must be compacted and levelled using a piece of wood or screed bar to smooth out any minor undulations. At this point a layer of shock-absorbing material can be put down to give the final surface a more cushioned feel, but this is not essential.

Finally, lay the artificial turf, carefully aligning and pushing it right up to any edges to ensure it cannot slip later on. The artificial turf should sit just slightly proud of any edging so you may have to add or take away part of the underlying layers if it does not sit quite right.

Once the whole area is covered, cut to fit exactly with a sharp knife before nailing or gluing the turf in place. Silica sand brushed in will have a stabilising effect and help stop the turf from slipping.

Upkeep is limited to the occasional brush over with a broom to lift flattened blades and a wash with warm soapy water if it becomes dirty.

MAINTAINING YOUR LAWN

LOOKING AFTER A LAWN

Now that your perfect lawn is in place and growing away merrily it is essential that you spend some time and effort to keep it this way. Tip-top lawns require plenty of time, resources and effort to ensure they retain their good looks, and even the wildest patch of grass will need some attention eventually to keep its shape and style.

The amount of maintenance required is obviously dependent on the type of lawn you want to enjoy, but it is a matter of personal choice and lifestyle as to how far you are prepared to go to keep your lawn perfect at all times.

Few people have the time or energy to keep a lawn to bowling green standard as many professionals have to do. There are, however, basic techniques that need to be mastered and actions that can be planned into your weekly list of housekeeping chores, and plenty of tips and shortcuts that will help you to look after your lawn as best you can.

Grass and other lawn plants behave differently depending on the season, as do most plants, and there are times when more needs to be done and other times when you can relax a little more.

On the opposite page is a graph of the growth of an average lawn in an average year. From this you can see that spring, summer and autumn are likely to be the busiest times, at least in terms of keeping growth under control. Taking the appropriate actions at the right time is the best way to ensure that your lawn stays healthy and good-looking.

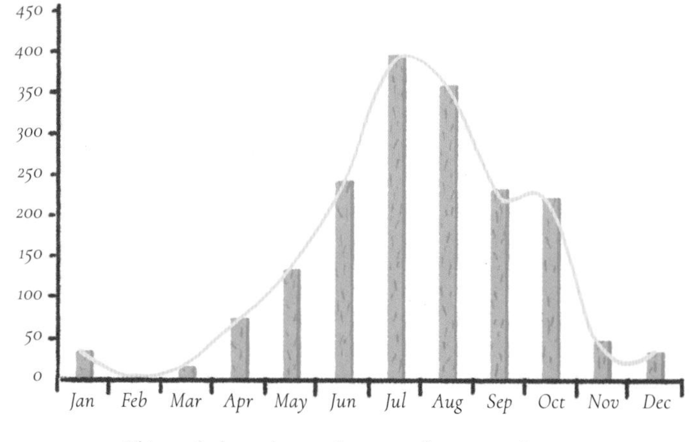

This graph shows the growth pattern of grass over the year.

Lawn maintenance can be as simple as a regular mowing regime or can be a more complicated activity that includes annual activities such as scarifying, aerating and overseeding.

Inevitably problems will occur on even the best-kept lawns, and methods of dealing with these are also useful to understand. Knowing how to repair lawn damage, recognising and dealing with pests and diseases, and good cultivation methods are all important techniques to have under your belt.

MOWERS

Choosing the right mower is probably the most important and expensive decision you need to make to keep your lawn in good condition. There is a bewildering range of machines available, from tractors and attachments that can cut great swathes of meadow and grass to hand-pushed mowers that are easy to use and need no fuel or power other than your own effort. For the traditionalist or history buff, any machinery may be anathema to you, so perhaps a scythe or billhook is the answer to all your dreams.

For most people, however, time restraints, budget and ease of use are likely to be the most important considerations when deciding on a type of mower, but there is bound to be something that suits you.

Depending on the size and type of lawn you have, it is worth getting to know the differences between the various types of mower.

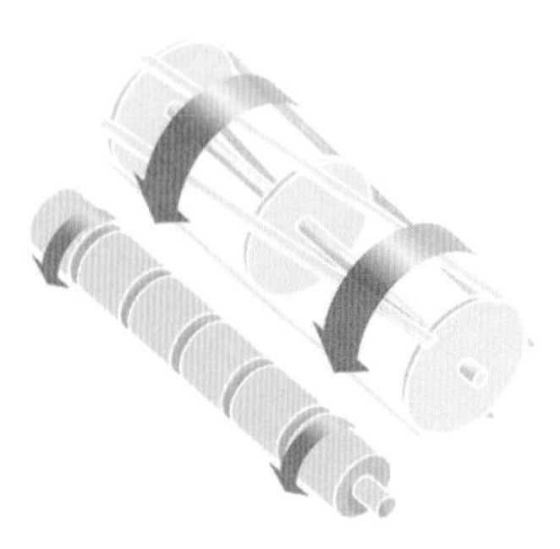

A cylinder mower cuts by trapping the grass between blades.

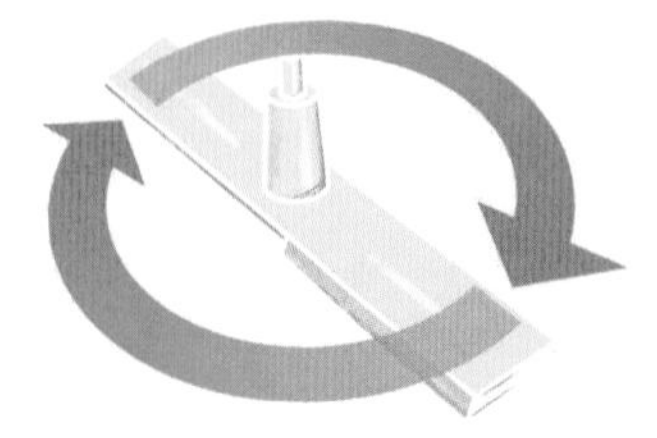

Rotary blades spin round at high speed, chopping off the grass.

Cylinder mowers

Cylinder mowers have a cylindrical structure that sits horizontal to the ground with a series of blades that move as the machine goes forward. Grass blades are trapped and cut against a bottom static blade. This produces the finest cut and is most suitable for a formal lawn or a high-quality sports pitch. Rollers on the back of these machines are often added to promote the classic striping that marks a well-cut lawn.

Small cylinder mowers can be pushed by hand. Larger ones require power to move them over the larger distances.

Rotary mowers

Rotary mowers have a blade that rotates at high speed, chopping the grass as it spins around. The cut is less fine, but it is quicker to use such a mower on larger, more utilitarian areas. These types of mowers need power to both move forward and to keep the blade moving. They too can produce excellent stripes if a roller is attached to the back. They are also the easiest to adjust to different cut heights, as this usually only involves changing the height of the wheels via a simple lever rather than making time-consuming mechanical adjustments.

Hover mowers

Like rotaries, hover mowers also cut with a rotating high-speed blade. Their manoeuvrability means they are well suited to cutting oddly shaped lawns and slopes, although the cut is rarely as fine as with cylinder and rotary mowers. Hover mowers need power both to turn the blade and to hover just above the grass level.

Both rotary and hover mowers can come with either a metal blade, in larger models, or, in less powerful machines, with small, detachable plastic blades that are easy to replace.

Power

A manually pushed cylinder mower requires nothing more than a bit of effort on the part of the gardener and is perfectly suitable for small lawns. For bigger lawns either an electric or petrol-driven mower is a better bet. Electric mowers are restricted by the length of their leads and their proximity to a power source, and leads are a risk if not kept out of the way, while petrol mowers can handle larger areas and areas not in the vicinity of an electric point but are costlier in terms of fuel consumption. They also require a modicum of mechanical knowledge to remain in good condition. Ride-on mowers for big areas of lawn are inevitably fuelled by petrol.

Modern battery-powered machines are now gradually coming onto the market.

Basic maintenance

A few regular basic checks and actions will help keep your mower in good order and make mowing easier:

* Read the manual before using and follow safety advice
* Clean the machine after every use before grass and debris have a chance to harden on.
* Check all nuts, bolts and fixings every time you use your mower, especially for anything wrapped around the blades.
* On petrol machines check the oil and fuel levels before starting the machine. Clean debris from any air filters.
* Have any blades sharpened when necessary. If you have your machine serviced this can be done by a mechanic, but you could do it yourself if you are confident.

LAWN CARE TOOLS

Strimmer

For difficult areas and coarse grass with weeds a strimmer or brush cutter for really tough jobs is useful and versatile. Some even have swivelling heads, which allow for quick lawn edging. The cut is not at all fine, but speed more than makes up for it in most cases. Strimmers are useful close to walls and other obstacles that impede a mower.

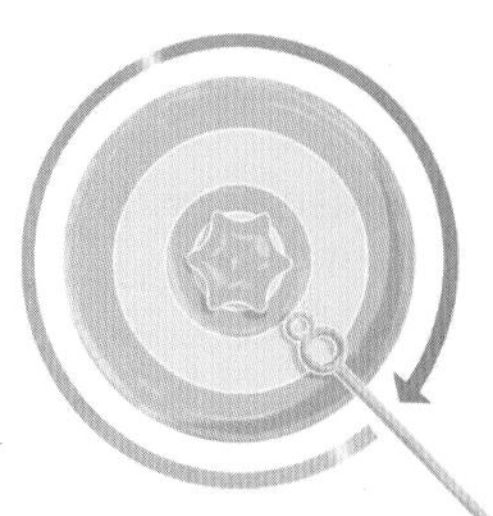

Strimmers have a plastic blade or line which chops grass as it spins round.

Scythe

Used for centuries before someone got round to inventing the mower, the scythe is a tool that requires precision and experience to create a level sward. If you are prepared to practise you may find it the perfect tool for your needs. The billhook is a smaller-handled version used where the great sweep required by a scythe would be inappropriate.

Edging shears

Designed specifically for edging lawns accurately, edging shears are effectively long-handled scissors that help you to achieve a professional and tidy finish.

Edging iron

Sometimes called a half-moon due to its shape, the edging iron is a specialist tool for cutting turf and shaping lawn edges. Used with a string and a plank it can create very accurate straight lines.

Lawn rake

Lawn or spring-tined rakes are different from the rigid rakes used elsewhere in the garden, with more tines or points that have some 'give' in them. They are used for clearing leaves and debris off lawns without causing damage, as well as to scratch off moss and thatch.

Landscape rake

This is a larger version of the standard garden rake, useful for levelling large surfaces quickly.

Turfing iron

The turfing iron is a specialist spade-type implement that slides horizontally under turf, making it easier to lift.

Besom

The traditional brushwood broom, often called a witches' broom, used to clear away leaves and debris from lawns as well as for working in top dressing and clippings.

Specialist tools for lawn maintenance

Specialist tools for lawn maintenance include the following:

* Seed and fertiliser spreaders.
* Scarifier: mechanical tool to remove thatch.
* Slitter: mechanical means of cutting down into the soil to improve aeration.
* Hollow tiner: this removes small plugs of soil to improve aeration.
* Switch: a long, extended rod whipped over the surface of wet grass to dislodge dew and prevent fungal diseases.

MOWING BASICS

Regular mowing of your grass lawn will not only keep the garden looking tidy, but will also encourage new growth and stronger roots, essential for drought resistance. It may also help prevent a build-up of pests and diseases, and will stop many weeds from taking hold.

Mow regularly and often for the best results, to avoid placing too much stress on the grass. This is the best way to ensure you end up with a thick, healthy sward, making it a pleasure to walk on. Try to remove around a third of the growth each time.

The standard mowing technique for a rectangular or square lawn is to cut round the outside edge first, allowing enough width to be able to turn your mower round before cutting the middle straight up and down, turning 180° as you reach each strip's end.

Once the centre has been completed, mow the outside edges once again, to clean up any missed patches caused by the turning process. Often this 'finishing strip' has to be double width for larger machines.

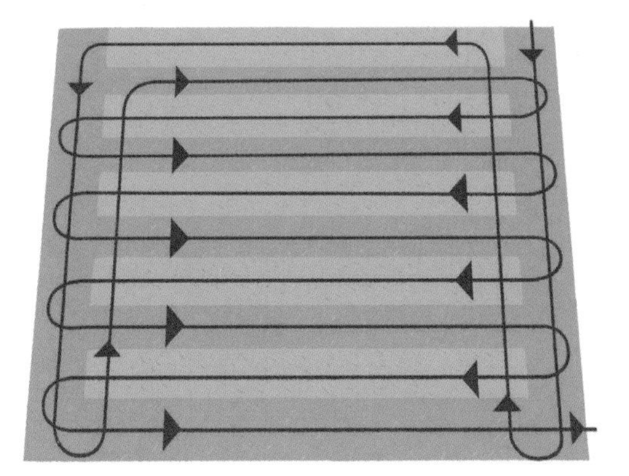

Follow this classic mowing pattern for a professional result.

It is important to remember that the cutting area of your mower is likely to be less than the width of the machine itself, so you must overlap a little or you will end up with small strips of uncut grass in between the mown ones.

With a roller on the back of your mower your lawn should end up with beautiful stripes: these are a result of the grass being rolled forwards in the direction in which the mower has travelled.

Curved and irregular areas need to be planned out a little differently, especially for neat stripes. Start by mowing the outside edge then mow the middle, starting at the centre and mowing one half first before returning to the centre and mowing the other half. Alternatively, remove the roller completely or use a hover mower to cut it.

Changing the direction you mow on a regular basis will stop ridges from forming. This is particularly important to prevent 'graining' on sports turf, which occurs if the same direction of mowing is used each time, forming ridges and patterns that affect the way the balls run.

How often and how high?

The answer to this question depends partly on the quality of your lawn and its use, as well as the season.

High-quality turf needs mowing most frequently to maintain its appearance and is usually cut much lower during the peak growing season for the same reason. Utility lawns may be kept a little longer and are cut fewer times to cushion some of the effects of high traffic and the wear and tear of outdoor life. Rough grass can be cut less frequently still.

Disposing of cuttings

All this cutting means that the thorny subject of what to do with the clippings will raise its head every now and again. It is possible to buy mowers that have extra blades that cut up the clippings finely and deposit them back on the grass to fertilise the lawn naturally, known as 'mulching' mowers, but these are not commonly available. Theoretically, grass clippings left on lawns will provide over 50 per cent of your lawn's nitrogen needs as well as a range of other nutrients and minerals. They can also help minimise water loss by acting as a thin mulch. The downside is the mess this can create, as clippings stick to shoes and paws and are tracked back into the house or spread over paths. They can also spoil the striping effect and general neat look of a fine lawn.

Collecting clippings in a special box attached to the mower is a possibility with cylinder and rotary mowers. This is usually standard for finer lawns, discouraging earthworm activity and the spread of weeds and possibly preventing a build-up of thatch as well. Without a box to collect clippings you may have to hand rake any large amounts of clipping debris to prevent the grass underneath from suffering through lack of sunlight.

Clippings can be used on the compost heap, unless weedkiller has recently been applied, although it should be sprinkled over in layers, preferably when dry. Applied in one bulky package the nitrogen content in grass will quickly result in a smelly, ammonia-rich, slimy lump, so do mix it with plenty of brown, carbon-rich plant debris to avoid any unpleasantness. Alternatively, it can be used as a mulch on potatoes in the vegetable garden to reduce the likelihood of potato scab, or even laid over cardboard on paths to act as a weed suppressant.

WATERING AND IRRIGATION

Water is essential to all life. However, grass has an amazing ability to survive periods of drought, although it may not look attractive during an especially dry spell. In most cases, no matter how bad things get, it will start to recover as soon as cooler temperatures and rainfall return, especially if the initial preparations were good and the grass reasonably well maintained.

Due to its biology some types of grass can even survive fires, recovering quickly and feeding off the nutrient-rich ash that is left behind. Indeed, in some parts of the world burning grass in spring is considered an essential part of the annual lawn maintenance programme, following the centuries-old tradition of managing prairies and savannahs with clearance fires. This is not, however, to be recommended, as it destroys wildlife habitats, pollutes the atmosphere and causes unintended, often out-of-control bush fires wherever the practice is prevalent.

It is a reminder, however, that all is not lost if, as is so often the case, a dry period results in a hosepipe ban or the rationing of water supplies. Grass may turn brown and look dead but is actually simply dormant. Given the consequences of climate change, with its increasing temperatures and extremes, we may have to get used to periods when our lawns will simply not look as lush as we would like.

The one time when watering and irrigation are essential is just after the formation of a new lawn. Germinating seeds and seedlings are easily killed due to lack of water. Once the lawn

Different types of sprinkler are available to help keep your lawn green and fresh.

is established, however, irrigation is only required during dry, hot seasons and only if watering is not restricted.

For a very small area you can use a watering can with a rose attached, as long as you use enough water to penetrate deep into the soil. Shallow watering will do more harm than good, forcing roots closer to the surface and leaving grass more exposed to drought than ever.

In most cases lawns are big enough to justify the use of hosepipes. Watering a lawn of any size is a chore for almost anyone so should only be undertaken when the grass fails to spring back after being walked upon, indicating it is in need of moisture. Early morning or evening are the best times to water in order to minimise losses due to evaporation. The lawn needs to be thoroughly wetted to a depth of at least 10cm (4in) to be worthwhile. To be sure, use a spade or trowel to take out a long plug or square in the least noticeable part of your lawn and check to see how far down the water has penetrated – moist soil will be darker. Alternatively, buy a soil moisture sensor, and insert the probe carefully into the lawn in several places to test the moisture content below.

On heavy soils, pooling on the surface may indicate a problem with drainage, resulting in roots being starved of essential oxygen. In this case reduce the frequency of watering and consider improving the drainage. Sandy soil will need more water than heavier clay soils.

For large areas of lawn some sort of sprinkler system may be more suitable. Various types are available: static sprinklers usually spray in a circle; oscillating sprinklers spray from side to side; while rotary arm sprinklers turn through 360°, covering a wider area. A pulse jet sprinkler usually has the most efficient and widest reach. Whichever type you choose, try to place it so that water is not wasted unnecessarily.

Use a daisy grubber to yank weeds out at the root.

WEEDING

A few weeds in your lawn may be rather charming, so unless you want a perfectly manicured lawn there is no need to worry too much. There is, after all, a simple delight in making a daisy chain or blowing a dandelion clock on a sunny afternoon. So think before grabbing a bottle of weedkiller at the first sign of intruders.

For formal lawns, however, anything that mars that impeccable sward can easily ruin the overall effect. Even regular mowing may not deter certain weeds, as some, such as daisies and dandelion, will adapt, growing back flatter and smaller to ensure survival.

There are also good practical reasons to keep on top of weeds. Many will outcompete grass and, if left, could take over completely, as well as colonising the rest of the garden. Dandelion clock-blowing does have its consequences. There are even a few unpleasant weeds, such as thistles and nettles, which can actually hurt garden visitors if left unchallenged.

Weeding by hand

For one or two odd weeds a long, thin trowel, known as a daisy grubber, will reach far enough down to remove weeds without too much disturbance. Alternatively an old kitchen knife will do the job almost as well. Don't use a good knife as the grit and soil will quickly ruin it.

Using weedkiller

Spot weeding using a paint-on selective weedkiller is an option, or, failing that, a standard systemic weedkiller such as glyphosate, though this will also kill nearby grass if not applied carefully.

For more infested lawns a broadleaf weedkiller may be required. This type of herbicide has been developed to destroy leafy plants but has no effect on grass itself if used correctly. A stand-alone selective weedkiller is preferable to those products advertised as 'weed and feed' from an environmental point of view, as it is only applied when you need to kill weeds rather than several times a year.

It is extremely important to be accurate with any kind of chemical product like this and follow the instructions carefully. Too concentrated and over-applied and the grass may also be killed. Too weak and it will not do its job correctly and you may be tempted to reapply it, increasing the environmental damage. Never be tempted to add a bit extra just to be on the safe side. It's probably better to tolerate a live weed than end up with dead grass.

Selective weedkiller is available in a variety of forms. Concentrated products that have to be mixed with water are usually the best value, but pre-mixed is easier to apply and removes the complications of accurately measuring and mixing. Dry granules, too, are easy to apply as long as you use a spreader, properly calibrated.

If using a liquid weedkiller, smaller lawns can be successfully treated with a watering can and a sprinkler bar, but a knapsack sprayer, like the ones used by professionals, may be useful for larger areas. To avoid over-applying weedkiller or missing sections, use canes and string as guidelines and be methodical. Matching the distance between your string to the length of your sprinkler bar or knapsack spray width will help enormously.

Always use weedkillers properly and safely, and preferably only as a last resort.

Organic grass care

Dealing with large amounts of weeds in grass is one of the more tricky problems to handle if you prefer chemical-free gardening. Accepting a level of weeds in your grass may be a necessary trade-off. If regular hand weeding does not control the problem, it may be better to start again, replacing the infested turf and dealing with any weeds that appear thereafter as soon as possible. Prevention is better than cure when it comes to organic grass care. Organic weedkillers, based on pelargonic acid, are now coming on the market if you want to try them.

FEEDING

Like any other plant, grass needs to access a range of nutrients to grow well and resist disease. The three major nutrients required are nitrogen (N), phosphorus (P) and potassium (K). Iron (Fe) too is a useful addition. Shop-bought fertilisers will indicate the levels of these nutrients as a ratio N:P:K, so even if you are not using a special grass fertiliser product you should be able to choose a product that's right for the season and the condition of your grass.

Nitrogen promotes rapid, green growth, essential given the amount of mowing inflicted on grass, and more is needed if grass clippings are regularly removed. Phosphorus promotes root growth while potassium helps grass resist cold, disease and drought. Iron greens up grass beautifully without encouraging too much growth.

In spring, therefore, at the start of the growing season, products that contain plenty of nitrogen and iron are usually recommended. In autumn, less nitrogen and more phosphorus and potassium are needed, to help grass withstand the vagaries

Look for the appropriate N:P:K ratio when buying fertiliser to ensure your purchase will have the right results.

of winter without promoting too much leaf growth. Giving your lawn too much nitrogen at the end of the growing season will only encourage soft growth just at the point when it needs to be at its toughest, and can increase the incidence of fungal diseases. For most lawns a feed twice a year is more than adequate.

All fertilisers should be applied evenly to avoid patchiness and scorching. Granular fertilisers can be applied by hand or using a mechanical spreader, depending on the size of the lawn. As with seeding it is best to divide the quantity in half, applying one half up and down the lawn before turning 90° and applying the rest side to side. Liquid feeds work faster and tend to be high in nitrogen, greening up grass quickly, but are generally short-lived tonics rather than long-term solutions.

Chemical-free feeding for lawns is also possible. A mulching mower, which leaves tiny pieces of grass, returns nitrogen and other nutrients back to the lawn naturally throughout the mowing season. Pelleted chicken manure is a good choice for spring feeding, while bonemeal or mineral dust works well in autumn. Liquid seaweed is a good choice for adding iron and generally perking up your grass.

Ideally, look for a fertiliser that also contains mycorrhiza. These microscopic fungi colonise grass roots, forming a symbiotic, mutually beneficial relationship with it and greatly expanding the lawn's access to food and water.

Top dressing

Top dressing is usually a once-a-year activity that can also gently feed the lawn as it usually contains organic matter. See page 64 for more details on top dressing.

Too many leaves on the lawn will harm grass, so remove them when they build up.

KEEPING THE LAWN TIDY

Raking leaves

Come autumn, the leaves of any deciduous trees, climbers and shrubs will inevitably begin to fall and it sometimes feels that they all migrate straight to the nearest lawn. Beautiful though the sight and colour might be on a sunny autumn day, too much leaf litter can cause harm to grass, blocking out sunlight and air, and creating yellowing, etiolated patches of grass underneath. It also encourages earthworm activity. While worms are welcome, their casts can be unsightly on a lawn.

Where the leaf litter is not too substantial, mowing is a quick and fruitful way to clear the lawn. Both rotary and cylinder mowers will chop up leaves finely, even more successfully if you have a 'mulching mower', and the very small pieces can be left in situ, where they will eventually help to condition the soil. Larger quantities of leaves can also be mown over to reduce their size as this will help them decompose much more quickly, but it is probably best to remove them afterwards to a more suitable place to decompose over time. If you have a clippings box this is a relatively easy process, as long as you have raised the cut to its highest level to avoid too many grass clippings being collected as well. If not, or if mowing is not an option, it may be necessary to remove leaves manually.

Plastic leaf rakes are light and have especially wide heads. They are designed to reduce the effort and energy raking leaves can take, and may be a suitable choice for the less mobile, while being gentle on the turf beneath. Professionals, however, prefer to use a metal spring-tined rake, which scratches the soil during the raking process, bringing up thatch, thus killing two birds with one stone.

Rake the leaves into smallish piles before collecting and removing them straight away, to avoid any further damage to the lawn. Two hand-held boards used as a scoop is an excellent and cheap way to collect large amounts of leaves in one go, but you may prefer the large plastic hands sold in garden centres or a long-handled scoop, designed to minimise bending and straining your back.

Leaves gathered up in this way can be added to the compost heap but will take longer to break down than the rest of the contents. It is far better to keep the majority separate and to make your own leaf mould. Leaf mould makes a superb soil conditioner once completely rotted down. Although fallen leaves contain few nutrients, most having been pulled back by the tree or plant ready for reuse the following season, leaf mould is excellent for opening up the structure of soil and increases the water retention capacity by as much as 50 per cent. It also has benefits in terms of encouraging more soil life, providing a better habitat for beneficial bacteria and earthworms, which in itself will increase soil fertility and condition even further.

Depending on quantity, place the collected leaves in bin bags or dumpy bags or build a pen with posts and chicken wire to hold larger quantities. If the collected leaves are dry, water them gently as this will help speed up the decomposition process. Pierce holes in the sides of the bags to let essential air in before storing the bags somewhere shady and out of the way. It takes one to two years for full decomposition to take place, so check every now again, water if dry and give the bags an occasional shake.

Leaf mould that is ready to use will be black and crumbly and smell rather wonderful. It can be dug into poor soil, used as a mulch around woodland plants and strawberries, or sieved to make a useful potting compost.

Switching

Switching is still often undertaken by greenkeepers and sports turf specialists, though rarely by anyone else but the most committed of amateur gardeners. In spring and autumn, especially, dew collects on grass through the night. Left alone, particularly on grass in shady, naturally damp areas, the moist atmosphere can encourage the development of a variety of fungal diseases and other problems. Huge wide brushes are available which can be dragged across the grass to draw away any dew that has formed, but the traditional method is to use a 'switch', a whippy length of tubing with a handle around 4.5m (15ft) long that is flipped horizontally across the grass. There is an argument, however, that switching might actually spread any fungal disease or spores that are present and many people argue that it is better simply to mow when the grass is dry and keep the grass in good condition to prevent problems with fungus.

Scarifying thatch

Thatch is the name for the organic debris that builds up at the base of lawn grass. To a certain extent thatch is part of the natural cycle of decay and nutrient recycling as older grass blades die off and return to the soil to release nutrients and feed new growth. That it becomes a potential problem largely results from the tendency to mow regularly, which always leaves tiny pieces of mown grass behind, eventually building up into a carpet that prevents air and moisture reaching the soil and soil organisms below.

The build-up of thatch needs to be dealt with by scarifying, which can also help break up and uproot dead moss. However, it will temporarily make your lawn look awful.

Grass needs warmth, sunshine and moisture to flourish, so avoid scarifying in very hot, dry weather or in very cold weather. If the grass is not growing well before scarifying it will definitely not grow too well afterwards. Pick a day that is warm and dry and wait until the dew has dried before starting the work.

Cut the lawn the day before then vigorously rake the lawn with a spring-tined rake or a mechanical or powered scarifier. You can also buy or hire a machine to make the job much easier. The tines should dig well down into the soil surface to add air to the soil and to ensure that as much thatch is dislodged as possible. Gather up the thatch and any debris and remove from the lawn completely. To remove the maximum amount of debris, scarify the lawn in several directions and angles.

Springtime scarifying is not always required, but some gardeners do like to undertake a light scarification at this time, usually around April. In most cases, though, scarification is recommended as an autumn activity, around mid-September, to avoid spreading too many weed seeds and when the look of the lawn is a little less important.

Aeration

Scarifying the lawn will go some way to getting essential air to the roots of your grass, but should ideally be complemented by a specific lawn aeration. Again, this an activity that can be undertaken both in spring and autumn, although autumn is the more popular choice. Aerating your lawn will relieve any compaction resulting from use and will allow air to circulate around the roots and the base of the grass.

The simplest method of aerating is to spike the lawn with a garden fork. Push the tines of a garden fork down to a depth of around 7.5cm (3in), wiggle slightly to widen the hole and then move the fork 10cm (4in) away and repeat methodically across the whole lawn.

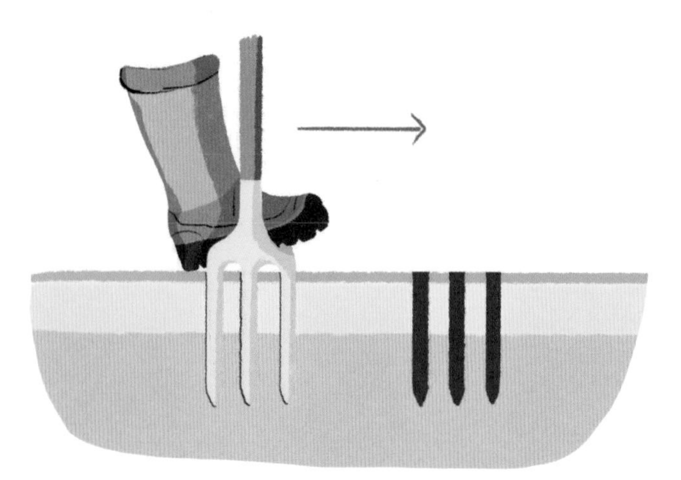

A lawn can be aereated using a garden fork ...

For more compacted lawns, a hollow tiner will be useful. Like a fork its tines are pushed into the ground, but on being pulled out small plugs of soil trapped inside the hollow tines are removed to be disposed of. The holes created allow air into the root area and can be later filled with top dressing to aid drainage and fertility. Hollow tining takes longer than forking as soil is actually being removed rather than simply moved about.

An unusual but amusing way to aerate your lawn is to buy a pair of spiked aerating boots. These strap onto shoes and have spikes on the undersole, which pierce the ground as you walk over it.

A machine called a slitter will perform a similar role, using a series of sharp, knife-type blades to slice through the turf and create airflow beneath. They tend to cause less obvious surface damage than other methods.

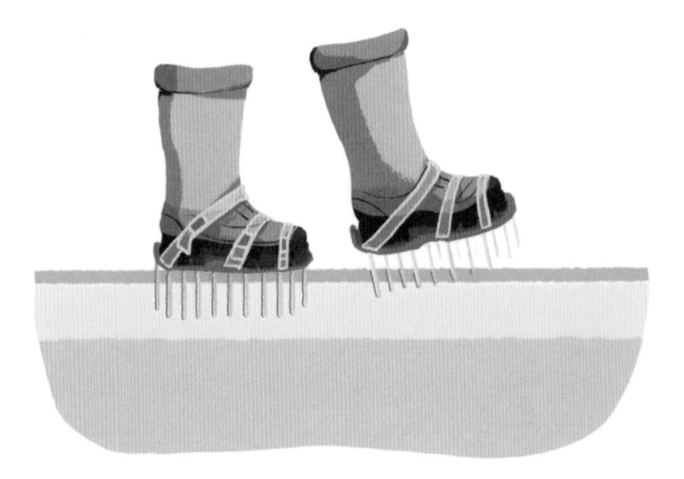

... or with special spiked aerating boots.

Top dressing

Once you have scarified and aerated your lawn in autumn, top dressing should be carried out immediately afterwards. Top dressing is a finely sieved mix of sand, soil and peat or preferably peat substitute. It benefits your lawn in a number of ways; smoothing the surface, improving the soil and drainage; and protecting grass over winter.

You can mix and sieve your own or buy ready-prepared products. The amount needed will vary from 1–4kg per m^2, depending on the condition of your lawn and time of year. Follow the supplier's instructions.

Apply on a dry day, either spreading it with a shovel or spade in a gentle flinging motion or using a mechanical spreader. Brush it in to distribute over the whole area as evenly as possible and water in afterwards.

Traditionally, high-quality lawns were rolled in springtime to resettle and even out the surface after the autumn's maintenance and winter frost. On heavy soils this could cause serious problems of compaction and is no longer recommended.

RENOVATING A NEGLECTED LAWN

Overseeding

Annual maintenance, weed removal and damage from use as well as weather conditions can all cause even the best-kept lawn to look a little threadbare in places over time. Spring or autumn are good times to repair and thicken up the sward by overseeding the bare patches or even the whole lawn.

Overseeding your lawn will not only fill in thin and bare patches but will also improve the colour and lushness of the lawn, as well as help keep weeds and moss from gaining a foothold.

It is also possible to improve the performance of your lawn by overseeding a specific seed mix to compensate for specific conditions, so if the newly built house next door is now shading your lawn you could overseed with a mix designed for shade, to improve your lawn's ability to cope.

Overseeding the entire lawn

Seed should be sown evenly across the lawn following the manufacturer's instructions, usually at a rate of 25–30g per m^2, and then cared for in the same way as newly seeded lawns.

If there are only one or two bare patches on your lawn, sow grass seed at the manufacturer's rate for seeding a new lawn just over these specific places. To save time, grass seed can be mixed with top dressing and applied at the same time.

Levelling bumps and hollows

Even the most beautifully prepared lawns may, over time, develop hollows or raised areas that spoil the overall effect, interfere with the pristine geometry of stripes and cause problems with mowing. Animals burrowing beneath the soil, constant traffic over it, heavy machinery or objects and weather conditions, especially heavy rain, are some of the factors that may cause these kinds of changes. Raised areas are likely to be scalped when cutting, especially in summer when the height of the cut is at its lowest, while the grass in hollows may miss out on being cut altogether. The end result is an uneven appearance to the grass.

Levelling minor lumps and bumps is easy. Using an edging iron, cut a cross in the turf, beginning at the centre and running out just past the affected area.

Fold back the cut sections carefully, using a turfing iron or spade if required, to expose the topsoil underneath. For raised bumps remove topsoil with a trowel until the bump has

Lumps and bumps are easily fixed in just a few steps.

disappeared and the surface of the topsoil is level once more before replacing the turf gently, firming with the back of a rake and top dressing the cracks. For hollows simply add rather than remove topsoil as necessary to achieve a good level.

Repairs

Small areas of lawn can be repaired in a number of ways. As described earlier, overseeding with fresh seed is one method, but if repairs need to be undertaken outside of spring and autumn you can also completely replace a whole patch.

Neatly cut a square around the damaged area with an edging iron and gently ease the cut piece off using a spade. Fork over the exposed topsoil, fertilise if necessary and gently tread over it to re-firm and level before placing a new piece of turf over the hole. Use a piece that is slightly bigger and carefully cut it with an edging iron for a snug fit. Make sure that it sits at the same level as the surrounding lawn before firming in gently and watering.

Fix damaged areas of turf by cutting out and replacing with new pieces.

Repairing damaged edges

Edges often suffer more than the centres of lawns. Overhanging shrubs and plants deny grass the water and sunlight it needs, careless treading on edges compacts and flattens, causing them to stretch out of shape, and in some cases the underlying soil simply crumbles or washes away, leaving the turf struggling.

If edges have become ragged, mark out a square section around the damaged area with string and cut out this section with an edging iron. Use a spade to cut under the turf and to push it gently forward until the damage is beyond the lawn edge. With a plank as a guideline, trim off the damaged section in line with the rest of the edge. Cut a new piece of turf to fill the gap behind, ensuring it fits and lies at the same level as the surrounding lawn before firming into position, top dressing any cracks and watering.

If new turf is not available you can also cut out the damaged area as before and turn it 180° before re-laying it. The damaged area, now well away from the edge, can be reseeded and top dressed and will recover in time.

If edges have become untidy and are out of shape, although not actually damaged, you can recut them completely with an edging iron using a plank or hosepipe as a guide. However, it should be noted that each time you recut your lawn will be getting smaller.

Renovating a whole lawn

All of these techniques can be used on a lawn that has been neglected, alongside a maintenance programme to improve the turf, although if it is in really poor condition it might be easier to remove it completely, rectify any obvious issues and start again fresh.

MEADOW AND LONG GRASS MAINTENANCE

One of the major attractions of a meadow, alongside its obvious beauty and biodiversity, is the relative ease of maintenance. However, to ensure that any meadow thrives year after year there are some maintenance tasks that need to be undertaken.

Despite their natural, uncultivated feel, garden meadows have to be controlled and managed to ensure that undesirable species do not gain too much of a foothold. The fast-disappearing meadows we know and love in our countryside are the result of hundreds of years of natural development, but this process is not feasible in a garden. Wildflower meadows usually contain a mixture of grasses and flower species, both annual and perennial, or even bulbs, but all types need cutting at least once a year, if not more. Cutting at other times can help manipulate which species thrive.

The main, once-a-year meadow cut, often called the 'hay cut' as it replicates this traditional agricultural practice, should take place in summer. For meadows that have been designed to flower more in spring, with plants such as snake's head fritillary and cowslip, this cut can take place as early as the beginning of July. Usually, though, the hay cut should take place later in summer, around the end of August, after the summer species have flowered and set seed.

Smaller mowers are unlikely to cope with the length of grass so small areas may have to be sheared by hand or scythed, if you can manage this technique. For larger areas it makes sense to invest in a strimmer or buy or hire a heavy-duty mower. Before cutting, visually check the area for any unexpected hazards, such as branches and stones, as well as wildlife. Hedgehogs are particularly vulnerable to injuries, or even death, from strimming activity.

Pick a sunny, dry day to cut all the grass and old flower stalks down to 5–7cm (2–2¾in) high, and leave the clippings on the ground for a few days to allow seeds to drop and remaining wildlife to escape. The clippings then need to be raked off to keep soil fertility in check. Remember that the more fertile the soil, the more unwanted, aggressive grasses and weeds will flourish. Collected clippings can be used as hay for animals or composted, as long as this is done properly to cope with the problematic remaining seeds.

In sites where grass growth is lush and fertility seems too high, or conditions mean that grass begins to grow again quickly, the meadow can be trimmed again in late autumn and the clippings removed. Over winter, too, meadows can be kept trimmed with a mower at least until the first signs of bulb growth, if bulbs have been planted.

There is no reason to either water or feed a meadow at any point as this will only encourage the vigorous grasses and weeds. Most meadow flowers have evolved to colonise poor soil, to be tough in the face of hardship, and will not respond to the extra care anyway. Other plants will, though; unwanted weeds such as nettle and thistle are not just painful to encounter but can come to dominate and outcompete the prettier wildflowers, as can grass.

Individual unwanted weeds should be pulled or dug out or spot treated with a weedkiller as soon as they are noticed. Grass that is too vigorous and beginning to dominate can be kept in check by sowing yellow rattle (*Rhinanthus minor*) in August (see page 34).

Long grass

Looking after long grass is probably simplest of all. A 'hay cut' between the end of June and late August/early September is all that is required.

Scything is the traditional way of mowing meadows but requires a little practice.

YEARLY CALENDAR

JANUARY

Service mower and sharpen any blades.

Avoid walking on lawn in wet or frosty conditions.

FEBRUARY

Order supplies such as seed, fertiliser and weedkiller.

Mow grass (high cut) if mild conditions are encouraging growth.

Trim grass edges.

Treat moss towards the end of the month.

Lay new turf towards the end of the month if weather allows.

MARCH

Mow more frequently, around every 7–10 days (high cut).

Spring scarification and moss treatment.

Treat weeds.

Feed with a spring fertiliser to encourage stronger growth.

Lay new turf.

APRIL

Mow weekly (high cut).

Continue to weed and feed as required.

Sow new grass seed.

Overseed bare patches or thin lawns.

MAY

Mow more frequently depending on type of lawn. Reduce height gradually to 2.5cm (1in). Never more than a third off.

Keep on top of edging, weeding and feeding.

Keep newly sown or turfed lawns well watered in dry spells.

JUNE

Mow little and often.

Feed if required.

Move furniture and objects on lawns regularly to avoid damage to grass.

Keep new lawns well watered in dry spells.

Mow spring flower meadows towards the end of June.

OF MAINTENANCE

JULY

Mow little and often.

Keep new lawns
well watered in dry spells.

Mow spring flower meadows.

AUGUST

Reduce frequency of mowing slightly, especially in dry spells.

Raise height of cut to withstand extra wear and tear and dry conditions.

Mow long grass and summer-flowering meadows after any flowers have set seed.

SEPTEMBER

Autumn-sow seed.

Overseed bare or thin patches.

Mow short before autumn maintenance.

Scarify lawns to remove thatch and moss.

Aerate lawns and top dress.

Apply autumn feed with low nitrogen to encourage root rather than leaf growth over winter.

OCTOBER

Regularly clear away any leaves that fall on the lawn.

Mow if mild conditions are encouraging grass growth. No more than a light topping on a dry day.

Continue aeration if not completed.

Apply autumn feed if not already done.

Remove any objects from lawn to prevent damage.

NOVEMBER

Clear away leaves.

Mow if grass is still growing. No more than a light topping on a dry day.

DECEMBER

Clear away leaves.

Mow if grass is still growing. No more than a light topping on a dry day.

Avoid walking on grass in wet or frosty weather.

DOS...

Do take account of weather conditions when maintaining your lawn. Climate change is affecting the seasonal cycle enormously and it is better to wait for a few days for good conditions than religiously follow a schedule. Keep an eye out for signs that grass is growing whatever the season and keep it trimmed and tidy with regular cuts instead of leaving it to get too long.

Do remember the golden rule of mowing – little and often.

Do try to catch weeds before they have a chance to take hold. Apart from looking better, this will help reduce the amount of potentially harmful chemicals that need to be applied.

Do follow the manufacturer's instructions when applying any products to the lawn, as misapplication may do more harm than good. An excess may leach out into watercourses or scorch or kill grass while too little is a waste of money and may build resistance.

Do remove leaves and debris as soon as possible.

Do service your mower and keep the blades sharp to avoid accidents and to prevent the grass being bruised and torn during mowing, and therefore weakened.

Do edge your lawns even if you cannot temporarily mow for whatever reason. It will make a huge difference and look much tidier.

Do water new lawns regularly for the first few months until they are well established. Morning and evening are the best times to water to prevent too much evaporation.

Do leave grass a little longer during periods of drought and minimise mowing to avoid further stress.

...AND DON'TS

Don't cut grass too short at the beginning of the season. Reduce the height gradually.

Don't cut more than a third of the grass height at any one time.

Don't water too lightly. Shallow watering will cause shallow roots, leaving grass even more prone to damage from drought. One good deep watering is infinitely preferable to several quick waterings.

Don't water established grass in dry spells unless absolutely necessary, and obviously not if there is a hosepipe ban in place. It will recover. Better to conserve any available precious water for other areas of the garden, such as the vegetable patch.

Don't turn to a chemical solution immediately. Catch problems early and try to sort them out without recourse to harmful chemicals to minimise harm to the environment.

Don't mow or strim without first making a visual check of the ground – for dangerous objects that might harm you or your machinery, and for wildlife.

Don't leave objects such as garden furniture or toys on the lawn for any length of time. Move them around regularly and preferably store them elsewhere when not in use.

Don't walk on grass in frosty or very wet weather to avoid damaging grass and causing unnecessary compaction.

Don't overfeed with nitrogen just to get a better colour, especially towards autumn and winter, as this will make the grass too soft to withstand harsh conditions. Also, excess nitrogen easily leaches out of soil into watercourses, causing environmental harm.

TROUBLE-SHOOTING

WEED I.D.

Whether you want to accept certain weeds in your lawn is a matter of personal choice. Daisies and buttercups are plants that we are often quite tolerant of, with strong childhood associations, while clover is often actually added to seed mixes for its numerous benefits. Nevertheless, more formal lawns are usually kept weed-free to ensure they retain that perfect green, silky look. Ideally remove weeds by hand as soon as they appear and keep the use of chemical weedkillers to a minimum.

1. Daisy (*Bellis perennis*)
Probably the most common perennial weed in lawns, daisies are pretty much recognised by everyone. Their green, spoon-shaped leaves lie flat or near flat on the ground forming clusters of rosettes with short-stemmed, small, yellow-centred white flowers. They can withstand close mowing, simply growing more and more in a horizontal direction to cope, but can be removed by hand with a knife or the long, thin trowel known as a 'daisy grubber'. Alternatively, enjoy making daisy chains.

2. Slender speedwell (*Veronica filiformis*)
With tiny, round, serrated leaves, speedwell spreads by runners both under and over the ground, and produces a mass of individual, lilac-blue flowers with a white centre. Notoriously

1.

2.

difficult to remove from lawns as mowing simply chops up the runners, spreading them further afield. Hoeing can help, or use a selective weedkiller if you have to.

3. Dandelion (*Taraxacum officinale*)

Another recognisable perennial weed with edible, softly toothed leaves. The bright yellow flowers turn overnight into balls of white, fluffy seedheads, perfect for blowing all around the garden (and for telling the time, apparently). Dandelion has a deep, fleshy taproot, which must be dug out completely or it will simply regrow. Another weed that adapts to close mowing.

4. Yarrow (*Achillea millefolium*)

Yarrow's tough, feathery foliage releases a distinct scent when crushed. It prefers dry, sandy soil and has creamy white clusters of flowers. Pull out rhizomes by hand before it spreads too far.

5. Couch grass (*Elymus repens*)

Couch or twitch grass is a tough rye grass common throughout Europe. It has broader, tougher blades than lawn grass and produces larger, unsightly clumps and tussocks if growing in lawns. It spreads by underground rhizomes. Couch grass is best removed by hand, making sure that all the creeping rhizomes are removed too, as selective weedkillers will not work.

3.

4.

6. White clover (*Trifolium repens*)

A perennial, which may or may not be a blessing in a lawn, white clover, and its pink cousin *Trifolium pratense*, can spread via runners and smothers many lawn grass species. The flowers, however, are a valuable food source for bees and other flying insects, and clover, especially microclovers, is sometimes added to lawn mixes as it is resistant to dog urine and drought and remains green under almost every condition as well as providing valuable nutrients. If its presence is not wanted, rake hard to dislodge and lift runners before mowing closely.

7. Greater plantain (*Plantago major*)

Plantain has broad, dessert spoon-shaped leaves with ribs that will smother any grass beneath. The blue-green flowers are held on stiff stalks. Dig out individual rosettes before they have a chance to seed. Regular mowing will also help prevent this plant from seeding and spreading.

8. Creeping buttercup (*Ranunculus repens*)

A sign that your lawn has drainage issues, this is a weed that enjoys damp soil. Shiny yellow cups are borne above distinctive three-lobed foliage. The plant spreads via underground stems. Dig out established plants, removing all the creeping roots.

5.

6.

7.

9. Selfheal (*Prunella vulgaris*)

With pretty purple flowers, this is a member of the mint family, and like its relative can spread rapidly. It too is edible and, as its name suggests, traditionally used as a medicinal herb. Leaves are borne in pairs along square stems, while under the ground runners will help it spread throughout a lawn. Hand weed as soon as it is spotted, or use an appropriate weedkiller if absolutely necessary.

10. Common ragwort (*Senecio jacobaea*)

A weed that is toxic to both animals and humans, it is sensible to control this plant at an early stage as it is a prolific seeder. A biennial, with blueish-green, finely divided leaves, the yellow, starry flowers are borne on tall stems. It thrives in dry conditions and is more of a problem in meadows and long grass than in closely mown lawns. Dig out completely before it grows to its full height. Wear gloves when handling and avoid breathing in the fine seeds. Selective weedkillers are an option if the problem is severe, especially if grazing animals live nearby.

Bare patches in your lawn will encourage an infestation of ephemeral and annual weeds, such as chickweed, bittercress and groundsel, which grow fast and go to seed quickly. Keep bare areas hoed to prevent this problem.

8.

9.

10.

PESTS

Ants

Although ants are not considered to be particularly harmful in the garden, they may sometimes become a problem in lawns and meadows if their nests are large, forming unsightly hummocks that make mowing difficult. Their intricate underground burrows can also damage grass roots, causing yellow, dead patches to appear.

While most ants are harmless creatures, red ants do have a sting, usually no more than an irritation but still an unpleasant experience if you are walking barefoot, though red ants are more likely to be found in rough grass and meadow rather than manicured lawns. On the whole most ant species prefer dry, well-drained, sandy soil in areas where they are unlikely to be too disturbed.

Ant hills, made up of fine soil, a by-product of burrowing activity, can be dispersed over the lawn with a broom before mowing, and in most cases a weekly brush in summer will keep ant numbers and activity under control and avoid the use of chemicals. Nematodes are also available in the warmer months, which will irritate the colony enough to force them to move.

Leatherjackets

Leatherjackets are the larvae of crane flies or daddy-long-legs. These brownish-black tubular larvae spend the winter just below the surface of turf, voraciously eating grass roots and stems, leading to thin or dead patches, and can destroy whole lawns. Birds will peck at the lawn surface to get their beaks on this nutritious snack, creating further damage.

There are no longer any chemical control measures to treat leatherjackets, although nematodes are available during the warmer months. Regular checking in winter and spring is the best method of dealing with leatherjackets. Dig small test holes to check for their presence, or lay black sheeting out overnight on a small section of well-watered turf, which will encourage any larvae to come to the surface. They can then be removed and disposed of. Covering the whole lawn in this way is an effective method of controlling an infestation.

Chafer grubs

Unattractive grubs that look as if they are filled with custard, certain types of chafer larvae can cause lawn problems not only by chewing on grass roots but also by attracting lawn-destroying predators such as badgers. Larvae of the Welsh and garden chafer beetle are to blame, feeding just below the surface and often creating yellow patches in lawns, especially from autumn to spring. Characteristically they are curved in a C-shape with brown heads and three pairs of legs towards the top end.

There are no chemical controls available for amateur use but biological nematodes are available to help control them. These are best applied as a preventive measure in late summer as the pathogenic nematodes involved need a warm soil temperature to be activated. The soil temperature during the chafer grub's most active period is not likely to be adequate.

Miner bees

There are hundreds of species of bee, and the vast majority of them are harmless. So if you do spot tiny, volcano-shaped mounds of earth appearing in lawns in late spring and spot bees flying in or out, there is no reason to panic. These are miner or burrowing bees, with no sting but an important role in pollinating the rest of your garden. They prefer to burrow in light, dryish, sandy soil so are often attracted to lawns where they may cause a bit of temporary unsightliness.

Each burrow is the nest of a single queen, although often many queens may live in close proximity so that it appears to be a sort of giant, connected hive. Miner bees are docile and should be treated as a bonus, rather than a pest, as their burrows perform a valuable aerating function. If you do wish to take action, brushing the soil over the lawn is an option, or watering the ground may encourage them to move elsewhere, but on the whole it is better to just let them be. At the end of the breeding season the nests will simply disappear.

Worms

Worms are another creature that traditionally have been seen as an enemy of good lawn-keeping, though they are of vital importance to a healthy garden. True, their casts, the small mounds of curly, ingested soil deposited on the lawn surface can be unsightly, but the presence of worms in your lawn is an indicator of good health and should be celebrated. Worm activity in your lawn will aerate and fertilise the grass, keep down thatch and generally be a bonus to the garden's vital ecological systems.

In most cases the casts can be brushed or gently raked when dry and will naturally fertilise the lawn. Alternatively leave the grass a little longer to hide them. Worms tend to prefer more alkaline conditions so applying soluble iron, which is slightly acidic, may deter them. However over-application may cause too great a change in the soil pH so this is not a particularly useful option. Neither is worm-charming, although feel free to give it a try.

DISEASES AND DISORDERS

Red thread

This is probably the most common lawn disease. Grass tips will turn red in patches before dying off, especially in wet summers. It rarely infests a lawn completely, but patches can vary from a few centimetres across to 25cm (10in) or more, turning from red to brown or bleached out completely. The fungus *Laetisaria fuciformis* is responsible and is most active in late summer, especially on common lawn grasses such as fescues and bents. Red grass is a sign of possible nitrogen deficiency, so a nitrogen-rich feed will hopefully stop it in its tracks, as long as autumn is not looming. Damaged patches can be repaired by scarifying and aerating well, and overseeding at the right time.

Snow mould

Snow mould or fusarium patch is caused by another fungus, *Microdochium nivale*, which is better able to survive cold conditions, hence it is often seen after snow has fallen. Like red thread disease, its presence leads to patches of yellow grass, sometimes with a layer of white or pink threads just visible to the naked eye, and it can spread widely, even destroying whole lawns.

Dollar spot

Dollar spot is more common on golf courses than most garden lawns, but it is another fungal disease that might cause unsightly patches, albeit small, round, coin-sized ones at least initially. White mould may be seen on the patches on dewy mornings and following rain, especially on lawns with a high fescue content, although it does attack other types of grass too.

Sclerotina homeocarpa fungus is most active in summer and autumn, but preventive measures such as allowing the lawn to dry more quickly by removing overhanging branches and maintaining good drainage will help. Keeping up a good feeding regime and raising the height of your cut will also help.

Rust

As elsewhere in the garden, rust may appear on your lawn grasses, usually during the summer months. Orange pustules coat the individual grass blades, causing yellowing, but rarely actually kill the whole plant. There are no chemical controls available, but regular mowing will stop the spread of the millions of tiny spores that the orange fruiting pustules can release if allowed, and healthy, well-kept lawns should recover easily.

Moulds, algae and dog lichens

All three cause little real harm to your lawn, but may be slippery and are unpleasant to look at. They flourish in damp, shady, cool conditions, especially under trees. Algae and slime mould tend to look like lumps of jelly in various colours, while dog lichens are small, grey or brown, flat shapes like platelets. Improving conditions and reducing shade and dampness will help, but you can also try dissipating them with a good squirt of water from a hosepipe on a sunny, warm day. Moss killer may also have an effect.

Drought

Lack of water can quickly turn your lawn into the colour of straw, but with the exception of newly laid or sown lawns little lasting damage will be done, and it is wiser to use what water you have access to for other, less drought-resistant plants. Looking on the bright side, fungal conditions are a lot less prevalent in hot weather.

Starvation

Lawns that lack adequate nutrients will look less green and healthy than their well-fed counterparts, and will be more prone to attacks and competition from weeds and diseases. Applying fertiliser at the right times will help.

Toadstools

Lovely as they are, fairy rings of toadstools that appear almost overnight can be irritating in the middle of a well-kept lawn. Over time they will expand outwards and can remain a presence in your lawn almost indefinitely. Depending on the species of fungus involved, they may cause both luxuriant grass growth and the death of the grass immediately around them, which will be visible even if the fruiting spores are not. No chemical controls are available to amateur gardeners so the only method is to remove the turf and soil from beneath the ring and replace it entirely, although this is rarely successful as the underground parts of the fungus spread much further than one would imagine.

Moss

For some gardeners moss is the most annoying of lawn problems. It thrives in a wide variety of situations, outcompeting grass wherever conditions are less than ideal. Compaction, shade, damp, drainage and poor mowing techniques will all weaken grass and favour the establishment of moss, sometimes even replacing the grass completely. Controlling moss is therefore about practising good lawn maintenance techniques and helping the grass to flourish without giving moss a foot in the door.

Moss plants are made up of tiny, feathery, leaf-like strands that can dry out quickly in hot conditions but survive better when nestled down in grass, which protects them from desiccation.

Keeping the lawn scarified, aerated and healthy will help prevent moss problems, but occasionally you may need more drastic measures. Lawn sand (a mix of sulphate of ammonia, iron sulphate and fine sand) or specific moss-killing products are available, which, when carefully applied, can kill moss in established lawns, although the problem will return if conditions are not improved.

The best time to apply a moss killer is usually April, before the moss starts to produce spores, and September, giving you time to sort out any contributing lawn problems and overseed or re-lay turf. Leaving bare patches in a lawn for too long will only cause problems.

Moss-killing products are traditionally based on iron sulphate. Some are marketed exclusively as a treatment for moss and can be applied in autumn, while others also contain extra fertiliser like nitrogen so should only be applied in spring.

Lawn sand is often recommended as a solution for moss control. It is a mix of iron sulphate, sand and added fertilisers and works well if applied in the right quantities and in the right conditions, but any kind of mistake can easily cause a great deal of harm to the grass itself, so take care in its application. It can also burn the feet of any animals that walk on it after application as it is slightly corrosive. Typically iron sulphate will cause temporary blackening of the lawn, although this will disappear over time.

Organic or chemical-free products for dealing with moss are now increasingly widely available. Based on pelargonic acid, extracted from plants, they are quick to work, even in low temperatures, and effective, although they may cause some temporary scorching. They have the added benefit of being safe to use around children, pets and wildlife.

Whether you use a chemical or an organic product, do scarify the moss before applying to ensure that it penetrates to the base, and rake off all the dead moss a few weeks after application or it may contribute to the problem of thatch.

Lawns are also useful for cats to snooze on!

ANIMALS

As if the variety of lawn-specific problems and diseases was not enough, there is a strong chance that you will have to deal with some larger, better-known creatures at some point or other. Four-legged or two-legged, burrowers or top-dwellers, they can be a real issue for grass areas, especially high-quality ones.

Cats and dogs

Aside from the problem of cats using your newly sown lawn as a litter tray, the main issue is urine. Cat and dog urine contains high quantities of uric acid and nitrogen, which burn grass roots leaving browned off, dead patches, wherever they have been. Dogs produce more urine than cats but both cause similar damage.

The best method of dealing with the problem is to water the patch of urine-soaked grass immediately to dilute the acid and stop it scorching. Realistically, however, this isn't usually possible. Products are available that are designed either to be applied direct to grass to minimise the effects of urine or given to the offending animal as a tablet or a liquid to neutralise the urine at source. Their effectiveness is a matter of some debate.

On the whole it is better to try and keep dogs and cats off certain areas and allow them access to others where the problem will be less of an issue. You may even be able to train a dog, although the neighbour's cat will resist any attempts at control, no doubt.

Dogs may also rip up turf or even dig holes while playing. Again training and realism are the only solutions, so just be prepared for repairs.

Badgers

Many people would welcome the sight of a badger foraging and snuffling around their garden. They are, however, capable of doing a great deal of damage to lawns in their nocturnal hunt for food. With their sharp claws and digging prowess they can rip a lawn apart to get at the chafer grubs, worms and leatherjackets beneath, leaving chaos behind them for the owner to find in the morning. As a protected species in decline, they cannot be interfered with in any way, no matter how much damage they have caused, and few fences will keep these sturdy, committed animals out, so good lawn cultivation is the only real answer to minimise their desire to forage. No chafer grubs, no hungry badgers. If the affected area is not too great, chicken wire can be pegged down over it, as badgers dislike the feel of the metal on their feet. The other possible option is to provide another source of food, which gives you the option of enjoying their night-time antics. However you will have to maintain a regular supply or they will simply go back to their old foraging ways immediately.

Moles

Invisible burrowers beneath the earth, moles too can turn a well-kept lawn into a battlefield overnight, with molehills, usually in lines, appearing above the ground as if by magic. All sorts of home-grown recipes and deterrents have been put forward for dealing with a mole problem, from fox poo to rotten fish to sonic emitters, but their efficiency is questionable. Try brushing up the fine soil of any molehills and using it as potting compost before repairing any damage.

Humans

The animals above are simply behaving normally and the damage they cause is just an unfortunate side-effect of successful living. Humans too can unintentionally cause harm just going about their daily business. Walking across lawns eventually causes compaction, as does playing, gardening and using machinery. A well-used lawn may need more maintenance as a result, although keeping compaction to a minimum by staying off it at crucial periods, on rainy and frosty days for example, will help. Leaving items on a lawn for any length of time can also cause problems, so tidiness is important. In most cases, though, lawns are there to be used, and a perfect lawn may be one that is a bit patchy but obviously well loved.

Lawns thicken up when grass produces offshoots and sideshoots rather than new leaves.

GRASS BIOLOGY AND GRASS TYPES

Grass is one of the most important families of plants on earth. Rice, sweetcorn and wheat are all vital components of our diets as well as being the main source of nutrients for many of our livestock. Grasses, or graminoids, exist almost everywhere but there are only a relatively few types of grass, true grasses from the *Poaceae* or *Gramineae* family, that are found in our lawns and meadows.

A true grass only actually has three leaves, one dying, one mature and one growing. An individual grass plant cannot actually produce more leaves as such but instead will produce new plants as offshoots or sideshoots off the main stem. This causes the gradual thickening of a sward.

Mowing encourages this process, replicating the browsing of animals on grasslands, the constant 'attack' forcing grass to constantly renew itself.

Grass species

Perennial ryegrass (*Lolium perenne*)

Rye, the most common grass found in temperate lawns, is tough and resilient, perfect for withstanding the wear and tear of sport and family activity. It is also relatively cheap though it grows quickly, meaning that it needs more mowing than many other species. New dwarf varieties have been bred that reduce the problem of frequent mowing and give a lawn a finer look, while still retaining the toughness. It is not, however, particularly tolerant of shade.

Annual meadow grass (*Poa annua*)

Usually by accident, being a weed, most lawns will contain a greater or lesser proportion of annual meadow grass. It often colonises bare areas of lawn, growing short stems with plenty of seedheads in a short space of time. Unfortunately it tends to die off in winter, so those bare patches are likely to reappear. It is relatively unfussy about conditions.

Smooth-stalked meadow grass or Kentucky blue grass (*Poa pratensis*)

Popular in the USA, this grass has a relatively fine appearance but withstands wear and tear well so is normally used to improve the appearance of perennial ryegrass lawns. It survives all year round, unlike its wilful meadow cousin.

Creeping red fescue (*Festuca rubra*)

The slender blades and creeping habit of red fescue are often found in formal lawns where dense, fine coverage is needed. It is both tolerant of shade and easy to maintain, requiring less food and water to look good, and, being slow growing, reduces the need to mow.

Browntop bent (*Agrostis capillaris*)

Bent grasses like browntop are often combined with fescue for formal lawns, being fine-leaved and attractive. Bents can tolerate low mowing but are also often found in meadow mixes due to their fine appearance and delicate seedheads. *Agrostis stolonifera*, creeping bent, is also sometimes used as it creates a tight-knitted sward.

Rhizomatous tall fescue or RTF (*Festuca arundinacea*)

RTF is becoming increasingly popular as its deep-rooting rhizomes help it to withstand drought, waterlogging and compaction. With climate change becoming more of an issue this grass will inevitably find its way into ordinary gardens as well as sports pitches and public spaces.

Timothy grass (*Phleum pratense*)

Timothy grass is a coarse, tufted grass that is very hardwearing. It is not pretty and cannot be close mowed but can withstand considerable wear and tear so can be useful in specific areas.

Meadow grasses

Some grass species are especially suited for meadows, tolerating low fertility and drought, while producing beautiful seedheads. *Trisetum flavescens*, yellow oat grass, does well in chalky soils, as does the wonderful quaking grass, *Briza media*, while *Anthoxanthum odoratum* flowers in spring and is largely responsible for the evocative smell of hay when it has been cut. Ideally meadow grasses should not be too aggressive or tall if they are being combined with meadow flowers.

Seed mixes and approximate sowing quantities for specific situations

Formal, high-quality lawns: 50g per m^2 containing a high proportion of fescues and bents.

Utility and low-maintenance lawns: 35g per m^2 containing a high proportion of dwarf perennial ryegrass and creeping red fescue.

Shady, damp, clay lawns: 50g per m^2 containing a mix of rye, fescues and meadow grasses.

Dry, sandy lawns: 35g per m^2 containing dwarf perennial rye grass and rhizomatous tall fescue (RTF).

Coastal lawns: 40g per m^2 containing perennial ryegrass, fescues, bents and salt marsh grass.

INDEX

aeration 62–3
animals 89–91
artificial turf 9, 36–7

bees 20, 83–4
besoms 46
biodiversity 20, 30, 31, 36
birds 23
borders 10
bulbs 35, 71

chamomile 9, 29, 30
climate change 51, 74
clippings 49
clover 9, 29–30
composting 49, 71

design 10–11
diseases and disorders 60, 85–8
drainage 12, 14

edges and edging tools 27–8, 45, 68, 74

feeding 56–7, 75
fertiliser 17–18
firming 17
flowers 31–4, 35 *see also* meadows

germination 21, 23, 51
grass biology 92

irrigation 51–2

lawn types 8–9
leaves 11, 58–60, 74
levelling 15–16, 66–7
long grass 9, 20, 31, 71

maintenance overview 40–1, 72–5
meadows 9, 18, 20, 31–4, 69–71
mind-your-own-business (*Soleirolia soleirolii*) 9, 30
moss 29, 61, 87–8
mowers and mowing 42–4, 47–8, 58–9, 74, 75
mowing 92
mulching 49, 57

non-grass lawns 9, 29–30, 36–7

organic gardening 17, 55, 88
overseeding 65

pests 82–4
preparation 12–18

rakes and raking 17, 46, 59
renovation 65–8

scarifying 61
scythes 45, 69
seasons 40–1, 74
seeds and sowing 19, 21–3, 31–3, 65, 95
soil condition 12–13, 59
species 93–5
sprinklers 52
stepping stones 28
strimmers 45, 69
sustainability 11
switching 60

thatch 49, 61
thyme 30
tools 45–6, 63
top dressing 57, 64
trees 11
turf 20, 24–8, 67, 68

watering 51–2, 74, 75
weeds and weeding 20, 53–5, 78–81
wildlife 9, 23, 31
worms 49, 58–9, 84

yellow rattle (*Rhinanthus minor*) 34, 71